SNOW QUIET

Poems

by

Jessie Kachmar

SNOW PRESS   CHICAGO

1976

Acknowledgements: Some of these poems appeared in *Choice, Port Chicago Poets, Poetry Northwest, Our Only Hope is Humor, Gallery Series,* and *Twigs.*

With gratitude to John Logan and William Meredith

With appreciation to Carlajean Ginnis for
cover design

Library of Congress Catalog Card No. 76-49326

Snow Press
PO Box 427
Morton Grove, Ill. 60053

TABLE OF CONTENTS

Japanese Flower Show

Room is large with stillness,
    subduing.
Guests defer, a bit mumbly,
Comments respectful, shedding awe
    before each offering.
Works on the table were posed early,
Perhaps at night, assisted through
An opening in the Lake Shore Club
By respectable demons.
Each floral study stands in watery chalice.
Ladies in kimonos and obis go across
The floor like gentle mallards skimming
    toward goal.
They stop before a wayward plant to cluck,
Fix a wild stem or a curve improperly
    addressing itself.
The instructor swivels bamboo shears
    on a stubborn branch.
One knows in advance,
    it doesn't stand a chance.
Even the far-outs show method madness.
Now people are in queue before demonstration,
Sounds, only the sucked-in breath of Japanese ladies.
Under the arch of pine and juniper,
Mums are restrained above bamboo,
Bowed, at invisible court to Emperor Sun

The Milk of Blindness

Columbus dwindled to dust
    in the rusted manacles
of a small world.
He scented the golden Indies,
    reckoned out the course,
placed his trust before the court.
Faith warmed the King and Queen,
    faith melted their rings down,
hoisted the three Santas,
    and the sailing men.
Fear blew in all lost sailors knew,
    in storm they ganged the Captain,
howling woe. World was a dam,
    they were fish rushing,
down over the edge they'd go
        everyone.
And so they fell down into unknowns,
    bringing them home. Voyaging
shone a gold whose face, whose promise
    came to seem a fraud. Now once
before there came one, Jesus, whom
    judges nailed to his claim
to save men. Again common sense,
    yet child or pagan told it.
Men can be saved, but faith alone
        knows how.

Sand

She was growing headless from the sand,
Young figure, grave and primitive,
Curved by a forsaken hand.
There were warm bodies on that beach,
Abandoned mounds of fruit,
But she was the center, fallen meteor,
Lonely as the moon.
Later someone found her, ravaged her mute sand,
And levelled her down from where she came.
Only her breasts outlined the dusk,
Pears glowing dimly, in violet dream

wraith of freedom

Precisely this
marvelous Egyptian painting
without perspective
reminds me
Julius Caesar is always arriving
and getting shot.
See how this handsome young Pharoah
in his mummy gown just out
of the sarcophagus is being escorted
by Anubis, the jackal-headed death god.
The king has eyes of wonder, unbound
anticipation. He's at leisure
to be led, a shade in the beyond.
The frenetic arrow of zeal
is nowhere thrashing the air,
nor the motes of his being pressing
through an hour-glass. Grind
is nowhere, missing one whole dimension,
motion and murmuring change, swell
of atoms, waves crowding each other,
for cover.

Anubis bares no teeth,
no more at scent. The snout
is closed and peaceful. Here
he radiates, comfortable as
a full moon. In that space
where no restless fervor urges,
no hunger trembles and prods,
the soul is weightless as a plume
without wind.

    Those ancients were already
beyond our heats, into the dark cave, belief,
with its own illumination.

To a Woman come back

Ten years you've been gone,
    an interim murmur
    between lowered heads.
Now you appear again,
    your Greek marble stunning still,
The looks that kept incredibly
    during the slow immurement.
Now you leave your card,
    nationally printed.
You intimate God led you.
Your face, that separate miracle,
    flickers yet
    above its clay pedestal

Mrs. Lot

They should have warned her.
Unlike the travelling men
on silent beasts, she'd spent
the quiet years behind doors.
Only the leather-bitten knew
the sands were grains of nowhere,
that to leave the known would be
a jump into the nameless; better
eyes closed, also nose.
She went along when told until
the pull of home turned her around
as if she were inside a wind.
Could she guess the devouring past
would roll tornado force on her,
already swept and helpless
as the tundra, anatomize her eyes
and then her form entirely back
into fine crystal, trimmed down
to witness, all blown and barren
as creeping sand

To Francis Bacon, Painter

Give us leave to weep.
     Your stunted animal,
held upright by his clothes,
sheds no hint of man's descent
and would be spared the memory,
still tender somewhere.
     How slight the gates of being
 that man can be driven from it.
     In our invaded sun, tears
must be hoarded up to be called
upon. Rain is ominous and the dry
is tinder. Knocking ribs go
to death under the stars.
     And the stars, which are the dark's
lonely thoughts, what do they say
     about burning?

Reunion

We gather under the grape arbor
At an ample table
More than a dozen of us
From all over the country now,
Alive, picking at barbecued salmon
Served on Spode, lively fish this morning
Brought on our host's native hook.

Warmed in the trembling gush of sun
Going down on the gentle water
Where ducks, yards below our table
On the grass, keep up their rough honking,
Will we, wonder, ever meet like this again?
The paths were staked out once and chosen.

There's a scent here over the evening
almost of Bloomsbury; of intermittent minuet
Through years with politics, never letting it
Really interfere; except for the angels.
Anne, once young and pure from Sunday School,
Now a dogged anchor, thrice beaten, robbed
By black boys, alone in her white house.
Still she sings Black Panther. Salute.
May ideals last.

Common sense is the soup most of us fell into,
Some early, some late. Those who corner choice
bait early, often seem to dine in state.

Picasso's Chicago Bronze

Madonna some call it
Maybe dactyl bird
    swooping from far sky spaces
Or deep earth history,
One slowly rising from metallic wastes

    Angel perhaps, not human,
Angel like those of Rilke,
Sweeping fear, awe near to terror
    from all untagged beasts,
Angel with supersonic voice,
Dread
    too close to the Golem
        which burst the walls
    of medieval rust
        to take all crashing in his path
    to opening.
Only her own bottom weight keeps
    that bronze on the pedestal.
A jet impulse could lift the hulk.
Wings have yet no clearance
    to unfold the visible.
Still that image headed for the sky
    promises a latency
Promises a motion we can't track
Only intuit

As if one day when all is leaping
     at a level
When forces of a universal finally blend
     into calm sea
One morning in the plaza in clear air and sun
There's only pedestal there.
The terrible angel with its galactic eyes
Gone,
Leaving aloft not even vapor trail
Only terror dissolved along the path
Of that insensate gaze

Cesar Vallejo

You shared, in common with your namesake
    general, an assassin. Yours
was slow, unseen. It was your life
    that snuffed you out,
your life you could not recover,
    your life which burnt you down
into a hospital bed.

'Cause of death, undetermined.'
    What else. Rare infection?
Terrible sight. Poor Cesar, if only
    You'd been smaller,
With less spare room, with eyes
    of the ordinary man,
Total built-in blinkers, one
    who squares the common shoulders,
Shrugs off whatever can't belong to him.

You were too poor to have a sense
    of property. You had to see,
finger, feel, you gave to all a residence
    and that devoured you.

My friend, my poor dumb Indian,
    that is consuming disease,
Allowing no reentering.

The Beard of Elijah

When I was a child
    I was full of longing,
I say a child
    as if it had changed.
My longing lodged once
    in the beard of Elijah
And his visiting us
    for our ritual spring.
We set out a glass for him
    filled to the brim
with wine, the holiday sacrament,
    that he should come and sit
with us and sip of the wine
    we set out for him.
Each year with my eyes
    I measured the goblet.
I opened the door, I flung
    it wide. I gave him his chance
every welcome to come, I willed
    him to come and sit with us
and looked for a sign through
    the brim of the glass.
That would have been for me the Sign,
    enough that he had taken
Drops of the wine, not that he had
    to coarsen the chair,

With his visible image there
    Only give me the sign he had been,
A very few drops gone out of the glass.
    The sign never came. The wine
Never flowed from the edge of the glass.
    So went all the world's holiness.
It remained with the glass what one
    had to guess, what one could
        never grasp.

Sahara

Living, a map of Europe.
land, looking the same from afar
It is dangerous to assume anything

Change is hatching,
sand silting in a desert under the wind,
slowly, almost innocently

Look, everything is decently divided,
there are borders, there are fences,
do not think because there is no pistol shot
nothing is happening, only time

Suddenly Sarajevo,
Your life heard something drop.
You can't get past the border
and that guard you drank with last
he is out of sight

To Bella Ahkmadulina's *Yelabuga*

(Yelabuga is a small, provincial town where the
Russian poetess, Marina Tsetaeva, Stalinist
victim, committed suicide.)

That thing, the one that killed Tsetaeva
    is not indigenous to Russia.
We have a yellow bugger
    in these parts too,
which, regarding sex, does not
    discriminate.
Men and women accomodate
    in killing themselves
     with regularity
    for the Yelabuga.
It cannot be taken by direct assault
    or any common weapon.
More muscle than brain, it
    cracks people with furry knuckles,
ubiquitous knees, flings them
    onto the cordwood pile.
Guile alone may bring the beast to heel,
    while smiling like Jack,
     the Giant-killer,
    using for a ruse the bean

Meeting

A salmon swam upstream
last night where he met me,
midstream, the point
of no return. He was companion
to my childhood then, when he still
brooded over all astream that floated.
Now he's beyond all that. His
calls are silent like the smoke
of abandoned Indian villages
where only stones are witness,
cairns for the buffalo. As
the salmon leaves upstream,
he'll shake his word to the bottom,
       a drying scale.

Here on these walls

    anxiety preys, hangs its lichen,
hothouse moss, rough as a tongue.
Whether to shut off the news or listen,
'74 squats over us, massive curve,
Nevermore, black gaunt, fur

Want of relief becomes a haunted appetite,
a hungry man followed by a spectral dinner.

Hidden elites now intend and punish.
The others thrash their skin,
grinding their teeth not only in sleep.
Even the longed-for night with its plush dove
is a runaway. This is the year
of the rocking horse that goes nowhere
but invades, invades each grownup room
with its painted stare, its vacuous motion

Midnight Ward

Cezanne would have got it right,
over and over, cubes of white,
brass from the ceiling,
gaunt and stiff as body sprawl,
each one looking to
    birds in swift light,
who each day fly in to stop,
    pick up bread,
then fly out again

My shoes need soling

      I notice suddenly
up here in this luxury condo
I can't afford. Half-listening
to features clicked off like beads
on a rosary, heaven glows brilliant
around. Till dawn shows that I, who'd
like to stay, haven't enough
for the entry.
      My bleached, bob-nose St. Peter
convinces me this is the home for eternity.
See how the view at sky-level, the blue
of the lake stay pure—excepting far shimmers
of belly. The lap spread's that dazzling,
I feel myself ready to fall.
      That P R man who kept twittering
the best things in life are free,
wasn't here where the air's at a premium,
or else he covered the apertures.

Listening to *Katerina Ismailova* (*Shostakovich opera*)

Everything is always more in Russia,
Farther, harder, worse,
Plodding all those versts
racked up between gaunt ridge poles.
In spite of public comfort stations,
inspiring pictures down the sub,
and streets whisked within an inch
      of their lives,
The brooms are as ancient as the babas
      plying them
And their babushkas.
It's cold shivering all the way to Siberia
and stations for the mentally unfit.
What in France or another country
      would be Madame Bovary,
in Russia is Katerina Ismailova,
Drawn out, twisted down a guttural moan,
To a shuddering plunge

IC Station

Last evening
I passed a relic on the platform,
Red-eyed, cheeks under stubble,
A bum who leaned his rags
Over a bench

'Got a light, lady?'
I flustered for matches.

He returned to me
Surprise,
A dusty ornament
Fallen between the tended altars
Of my life

Looking

They found her pale and thin; almost dawn.
She was wandering, looking for something.
She quavered, "I want to be the way I was."
They laughed, "Don't we all." Nothing impressed.
She looked, went out to look once again.
"Where will you find it, what was it, who?"
She only answered, "Everyone, oh everyone."

"What is this it, who took it when, what happened?"
She said, "It must be somewhere, it can't disappear."
Her eyes looked fevered, her fingers scratched air
Over again, then again that it should not deny her.

They took her home, there was one they could find.
Still she could give no answer to the questions.
They knew no more for what she looked than others.
She wept on and no one ever turned up any clue.
The way she seemed was just the way she stayed.
She insisted it was taken from her. When
They shook her, she went on crying. Finally,
They let her, like a child, dig among the toadstools.

23

In the Hospital

Night light is garish
Patients in robe and slippers
      pad the floors,
         lay furtive shadows
along the walls.
      They take their walks neat,
like medicine
      Mouths are crimped,
eyes pick out other patients on their backs,
      arms flung in every direction,
Hands balled in final fists,
      as if what mattered were only here,
as if patience were a sheet they lay on
      could some day lift away

To Joe B.
who killed himself

You didn't make it, man.
You had to wait and waiting
killed you. You looked spartan
at first, hoofing that scholarly
bullpen, hanging to a string,
till they kicked the box clear
out from under you. Career done.

What were you but an early tidbit
for the cold war, kindling tossed
to spark a spreading pyre.

Your dignity made meager nourishment.
If you'd put on a tin bill, gone out
to pick it with the chickens,
you'd have stayed close to the ground.
Chimeras you nursed for a comeback
never did come home to roost.

Americans have no stomach for
long marches. Promises, paper
extravaganzas have trimmed us gaunt.

What else can be said? This time,
whole hog, stays indigestible

drift around Venice

Venezia
Wave murmuring Atlantis
on whose watery syllables
gondolas lisp
and dip their prows
slipping past the ruined palazzi
sitting in their sackcloth

These mourning canoes
with their moulded figureheads
slide into penumbra
shelves closing
memory

Venezia
langourous
nipped by hounds
of air and spume
is already apparition
melting between her caves
and chambers
lucent dream
falling into the grotto
of her own coloring

Long Spring

The doc is losing her marbles
      one by one,
Dropping them down the horrible hill.
Her framed certificates hang
      slightly wrong,
Not likely in this world ever
      to be straightened again.
Everything that could go wrong
      has been going for years,
Inexorable as caterpillars.

She walked out on the best advice.
Her kudos have been shoes she's hardly used.
She hadn't a stitch of audacity
      to throw them out
Or trim her toes.

I stand by and watch, a clock
      at a battlefield,
Giving nothing but time,
      watching for her
As she peels stale hide in stripes,
Until she appears once more,
Slim and dewy in a snug and supple skin.

/

In the Temple of Amon

It's not bad to be a Cat
        in Egypt.
No doubt, you've seen the head
        of Nefertiti. She was flesh
only. Where Cleopatra walked, the air
        was Cleopatra.
Antony trundled after in her shade

He banished me from the chambers,
        (he threw my pillow)
more than he could do with her.

I saw her today, stepping to her vessel
for the final battle
when the sun at the zenith
with the sky for a setting
seemed an umber gem in a ring
for Cleopatra's finger,
purple sails fawning around her,
heady with her breeze. When
her craft turned slate on our river,
        my mouse went small

In the Beginning

there weighed
an empty balance,
plain and primitive and pure,
moving side to side on
a tide invisible.
no justice
held it
but a void
moved in the distance
by a will.
An empty hour glass spilled itself,
a slow vial,
began again.
The grains were sleepless,
implacable as eyes
to indifference, to mercy.
Attached to each a barnacle, an
expectation, incubus,
A cushion.
Not a solitary gaze looked down alone,
not a frame, not a climate, not a sky.
Starting to knot itself nearby
was a hemp,
and the exquisite pink
that would be a shell

Cover

My nose turned a disapproving blue once
reading of Catherine the Great's tour
inspecting how her loyal subjects lives.

Aristocratic haw and hemming pasted
a view of papier mache
for her to travel through; gilded walls
of the guided tour (now chronic institution
everywhere) past the prettied gates,
the painted miles of cottages.
Perhaps they sprayed a million dogs
to give the Empress proper whiffs,
never have a glimpse of ugliness
behind thin fronts, how all would look
once scenery went with the white-gloved
stage hands.

It was the ruse I hated. Students
throughout the world object. They howl
down all facades.

Now, give two sniffs for empathy,
and a bow for Catherine's ministers.
Who else to sit with pigsties
all these years?

Monet landscape

One animal is native here,
    a windmill hunched in a ditch,
arms flopping over the turnips.
    Sky roars up quickly
from the horizon, out again
    like skin pulled over a drum.
The farmhouse, shabby afterthought,
    is propped near gorging seines,
    bursting beets,
        blowing pumpkins,
    burgeoning lettuces

Bud,

the disaster
that was our love
ravelled
blood trickling
through the after

leaning goodbye,
your words curved a wreath,
of course, we
should see each other
once more

we never stopped.
Year in, year out,
you were dispersed
through all geography,
A tomb
my muscle raised involuntary flowers to,
an enforced spring,
as if penance grew
from ground through doom

as if forever was a word
the wind brought and laid
on the doorstep

and I, burning constant,
Smoke of your presence,
your absence

well,

        it struck me, rather,
streets merely lie there.
When everything turns upside down,
streets merely lie. They wait.
Maybe they suffer. They're not durable,
very. Winters are hard, all the ruck
of running things, wheels.

Streets are meek and stricken,
stretch out their holes and ruts,
quiet.

Streets are mum as mannikins
that have lost their hands

Return

I wait to meet my mother on the neat street
    inscribed with flowers and rolled lawns
        which keep away rebuke and memory
Here they do not hang their clothes in the yards
    to rob the landscape
There is a passion for niceness
    and the air calls as clear as the notes of a flute
The high sun, almost invisible, penetrates everything
Almost I can forget the shadowy man
    near my retina
I will not look
I am ravenous for peace
I can barely see over the trenches of silt
My lifetime is a sod that cannot yield up its grief
Yet I am a small parcel of earth cast out of my mother
It is essential to keep walking
    lest the long fingers of the dead
        catch up and curling drag us down
They want revenge and there is none
My mother walks, a slow inching from disaster
In her tread long ago I'd lie scattered
    among moles and underground roots
At war's end I was eager with services
    to trace her family in the Warsaw ghettos
She had right reasons
She had to inhale joy along with all her neighbors
The Northern coastal sun denies dark history
The precarious summer runs fast and pulls everyone with it
Each week they roll their turf
While the earthquake gets closer every year

Adult Education

No longer do I ask myself
Why I am teaching these old women

Though the view of them is not ecstatic
I don't examine it for mites

A clear view of mountains of the past
Offers no St. Bernards
to lead me out to greater glory,
Much less the brandy

History is a bowling alley
Where it's always just too late
To call back the shots

Autobiography

At five, a playmate said
God didn't love me

I thought it likely
Ran crying home to Mother
Who turned her anger on me

At fourteen
My faith went,
From watching the religious

God was a terrible opportunist
He helped those mostly
Who could help themselves

I have whispered to the pious
The world is a leaning Tower of Pisa
With God breathing on it

And shivered that He knew
I knew

Duet

Veterans of wind, sun and gamey maneuvers,
Your lips in from the cold are rough.
You rub a six o'clock stubble
Sticky as thistle on a well-worn path.
We've used each other hard at times,
Yet we've survived,
Twin shells, rough oyster bark
In every weather,
Even those we floundered through.
Even as solitudes, back to back
We're twin
Like clothes poles with a thin line
Humming through.
Clothes poles, offhand, are not
ethereal. But
Generations swing
Between

By Silver Griffin Light

Busy Mrs. Grundy sails up over the Styx
Under her flannel parasol,
Comes back again with a bottle of Lux
By merely flexing her will.
She looks over her bifocals
As Persephone's daughter struggles
In a pit of snaky tar,
Pluto's place.
It's been so long the girl
Has almost forgotten just who is he?

Everywhere.
Calendar tongues have worn down fingernails

On her way originally
She thought she'd seen,
She thought
Land on the other side
Beyond the thick veinous flood,
Bright green,
And studded with cockatoos whistling
Jewelled as crewel embroidery
Where the trees were all rich and amazed
As monkeys
And only the tigers mild
And the streams were opals
Clear to the brink
And wild
To be tamed by a look
By a foot

What was she doing where she was what?
Crows flew half-mast intangibles
Daily at the hour

She would skip and go
By silver griffin light
To where the golden gherkins glow
And drizzle their undulant honey
In rows of slowing amber,
Boozy mounds around the sleepy moon

Affluence

She lives, my friend,
    in the far suburbs,
        still not far enough.

Keeping up, in touch,
    fitted her like wrinkles,
Till the accumulation got to her.
Almost every day,
    Encroachment.

It came to be her finger
    in the dike
        willing the wild back.
There was nowhere
    an austerity she could welcome,
Plainness,
    all that being worked out,
        a ghost mine.

She attends her own feast,
    holding at bay
        the scavengers
Avid
    for what she has not

To the lumberjacks

When I met you,
Paul Bunyan rose,
a man, not a forest deity.

The way you stood four-square,
said your piece,
printed conviction.
You didn't need to demonstrate
your courage and your hardihood,
put on gloves against
a double-bitted cross-cut saw.
Your work tossed easy,
a 12 x 8 from the woodpile,
too much for the ordinary man.

You'd stay all muscle,
lean spine
as you looked any man
in the face,
smiling with your square-cut teeth
among those towering trees, Buster,
took off your cap for ladies, Mam,
and liked the little kids and pups.

You walked, easy granite on the mountain.
Thataway.

Altitudes

The day collapsed at sunset
over mounds of hills
like a circus performer slipping,
then crumpling still.
The night kept knocking on the hill
to be let in.
At that stout mountain lodge
of cross-cut trees, we were
invited guests among happy visitors,
their moods upright and shining
as the skis on the wall,
ready for the season.
Your smile looked quite natural,
almost as uniform as theirs.
They never guessed that day
was a parenthesis,
all that elevation disappearing
on Monday's ground

Lilacs

My daughter stands by the open window
Hugging her new breasts.
Sweet, stupefying lilacs on the old tree
Shed a nimbus of illusion around her.
I cast quiet loam on my memories
So that hers may grow.

Maternity Row

Back on the table,
feet in the stirrups,
    legs under the sheet a mountain
then a plain up to my face,
    face, a reluctant moon
that would disappear behind
    any cloud, I lie and wait,
Organ on a shelf, tagged
    under glass for viewing

Here's the gyne,
    blur swimming up under a white gown,
skimming the polished lake
of the treacherous floor,
covey of young medics splashing after.
Chief bald head protrudes with spectacles
    over blue marbles darting. He mumbles
to the clock in his mind before addressing
    himself to my mysteries.
He extends rubber feelers; pain is conveyed.
    He flips, back to me, inaudible comments
to the young docs, who catch words like fish,
    eyelids flapping.

In a store, I would be cleared off
    the floor somewhat reduced. Under
gritty lids I wait, wait for pain tides
    to cover my moon face, flood out
        the asepsis

Year of the Junta

remembering George Seferis

Brief gold of Greece,
Air,
Air, bracing but thin.
Back of the whiteness of the Parthenon
    a yellow dog without a pedigree
Whined for the demagog.
Coming on, he pitched the lands
to the furies. They tossed them around.

    Sun is constant, always polishing
the bones of men on those islands,
    bones, piling layer on layer,
eras settling slowly on each other.
    Leaves on the calendar change the years.
Between the Doric pillars, vapors of death
and treachery rise, certain as spring, as regular.
    Meanwhile, the water laps, quiet on sand,
transparently clear down to the stones, and
            faithfully blue

To Charles B.
> *on his 'kicking the bankroll'*

So you didn't altogether like
> being kept by a dame
Even with bonanza of an organ
> that goes out instead of in.

There was the danger she might turn
> you to a wooden Indian,
Now, or future

Even growing a zipper with only one key
> won't guarantee
Dames from the likes of you,
Not women's lib,
Least of all, love

One day

   in the middle of my life
I stepped out of my body.
It seemed I needed another to rent.
The old one was through.
It sat in a chair, mute as a bandage
    over the eyes.

I started in talking, charged
   myself up,
"Look, chum,
Good Bye.
Understand,
it's nothing personal.
It's just that I need
a new garage for my motor.
Someone may find you, stay
  for the duration."
It sat there burnt out.
I had nothing to say.

The Glass Widow

Some take dope or pills,
    I collect jewels.
For every man gone, I get something new
A rare pin, black pearls,
Bracelets, anything pulling
My eye to the glass of store windows.
My lips dry, then wet a little, looking.

I've got a tree of earrings
Growing in my room
Where it looks almost like Christmas
Or tropical spring,
The season for baroque flowers
In a travelling greenhouse.

Every time a man leaves,
I go on a spree. I could start
A business or museum. Alimony.

Going down the cobblestones at Capri
Or the town on the Cape at the Riviera
I hear the stares of the old women
In black, following me. They dig
Like little pointed heels. "Rich Foreigner—
American trash," they hiss and nudge
each other.

The pads below my ribs are getting flat.

When I go to dine, I wear my quattro-
centro cameos or garnets florentine,
at the top of my gown, so his eyes
won't hesitate on my quivering arms.

I'm still rather exotic
     like my collection
How long can hope keep me in trim?
The one I'd throw it away for,
The One I was sure was him.

When the solitary moon shivers
into my French windows, I slip
my jewels out before I go to bed,
sit and gaze at them. I put one
ruby in my toothless navel.
It seems to wink out with a hidden fire
I could borrow.

The moon with his custard features
frowns, like a Pilgrim in my high school
book, that day Jimmy picked it up.

I burned right to the spot.

I drank up from him that year
like from a secret fountain.
Before going, he slammed the door,
Tossed the glass-rimmed keep-sake
Slow and easy to me.

I went . . . married . . . money
it turned out to be.
To keep me in supply.

The permanent Revolutionary

He was a pre-war prof I worked for,
Part-time when I went to school.
He willed my generation Deprivation
not with malice but from the best
intent. He counted on 'us'
to make a new world, a mission
of transparently delicate health.
Daily he viewed me gravely
through a tube. I gathered satisfaction
was a threat, a sun to blot away
the geyser of my grievances.
A pair of new patents I'd saved for
and wore cracked an invisible egg.
They were recorded by a frown.
I turned leery, let a new slip
go hang for fear he'd sniff it
with his beagle nose and droop.
Any portent of improvement trimmed
the balloon of his hope. Loath
to be a barometer of political weather,
I had to leave my Raven for another Mentor,
less tender of my welfare, present, future.

then and now

Now that we are no longer young,
no longer have those years
of our gone wearing,
when we turned to each other like fountains
to be replenished and found our streams
in each other,
It's as if that gift we had was struck
by lightning, shriveled away.
What we had left was too hard,
too thinly strung.
We weren't light or lifted enough
to walk now with our bodies upon strands
    of web.
What faint lifts were ours could not hold.
We needed new ground, hard earth under us.
Blind, we were mired in a cave.
Year after year we walked on tar.
It wore our souls.
When we fell out by a chance door,
    youth was gone.
We had not the comfort of arrival,
only an unsigned stop.
Humble, our bitterness hidden,
it was still in our throats, deliberate cud.
We were like captives taken in ancient wars,
stopped with the fling of a crust
and the chosen drop of oblivion

Audience

Who's knocking there,
        who's asking into heaven?

I remember once, Job came banging in
        with the spell on him.
When I was occupied with the gaze.
He wanted something,
        wrapped up.
Every once there comes a knock.
Old Adam. I fixed him
        with a pretty one.
No more. I hardly bother.
An inch, they want a mile.
Any time there's hitches,
        letters and complaints like seeds,
Even with spring.
Letters file into the sea.
        It's deep enough.
Those rumbles lately. One yell to remodel
caught me when
I wasn't quick.
Got me to where I had my curious hand
        out to dressing the curve
Of the world. Taut fruit.
Till my better judgment.
That face mooned in, all question.
I ran. If the door had opened in
        instead of out,
The world might have been different.
Not round, I think

Lady of the Fire

She rises waist high,
well to the heart of the furnace,
a maiden with eyes the color of glowing,
    one who stirs and drives all the flames.
    Her tongue is a spit in her teeth,
sharp and crackling, arms rising high,
    till the thighs of her leap,
she's up in the roaring, hair all awhirl,
    high up in the air.
She's dancing, eyes go snapping jet points
    to me, she's holding her arms out,
flame waterfall lady. Now sliding away
    she goes, hiding behind floats
of her veils. Sometimes she comes to me,
    curling a finger, looks for me,
looks at me, straight through the grate.
    I'm here now and ready. My brows
catch hot embers and my hair and my eyes.
My luck's gone away from me. Away she is gone
    in the middle of flame. I call her name,
"Lady of fire, show me your face, call me again."
    Wickedly, all she gave was a glance
        of her heels.

In a year I have grown. The grate's too small
    for my frame, and that lady of fire,
she won't ride to me ever or call me by name.

Poem after a Pinter Play

I live in a two-flat
The walls will not keep a respectable distance
Between is thin
Sometimes the stairs fold up like an accordion
Strange things take naps on the porch mat
The Ming spouts plastic grown by a guaranteed gardener
An ostrich, maybe giraffe, lopes in
Yesterday a Fuller brush man came
He still sits
His kit waits quietly
Some day he may go away

Middle-Aged Spread

The others in the circle
    drink, sipping slow Martinis,
smoke at cigarettes,
    order fine French dinners.

I order celery conversation,
    turn it neat
as the white collar
    on a confirmed spinster.

Alone, I reel as if at the rail
    of a ship
departing from shore,
    everyone else waving at someone.

Space next to me is conspicuous.
    I tell myself
A man's an acquired taste

In a scant room

Half-asleep,
my whispering arms reach out
for you, speaking,
but not out loud,
for it is only a dim impress
letting me know you are now here
and will come to me,
even with eyes closed,
hardly seeing,
through your hair,
through the dark,
through all the hulks rising up,
thrusting their weight,
all their awkwardness between.
It's not lightly I speak so,
not a matter of months,
or convenience or lizard indolence,
but of flowers that grow themselves
up between rocks,
continue and stand so,
looking out beyond dust,
whether seen or unseen.
There are their roots.

Widow regrets

I couldn't swallow
        tawdry—
        virtue prevailed—
    in solitary
There I assigned myself
        starving my bone talent
          for body love

I still hear that motif
        the moon sings to herself—
          enthralling shore

From my cell,
      it feeds worms
        to the sensual

Too late

I can contemplate forever
        the marble of my virtue
    and take it with me

The Specialist

'Our case is without hope . . work . . work.'

— Chekhov

Anton, you should have waited for that man
    who took his withered arm with him,
resting on red velvet in a customed case.
      It's curious, very curious, he said often.
To see how it would go, kept him waiting.
      The coast, downhill, compelled.
To watch it slide, for him seemed good
      as anything at all. Sentiment stirred
for what had moved, had once been lively
      with him, springing, faithful as Dunc,
          his pet retriever.
      In time he came to be authority
on muscles of the upper arm, was called
      The Arm in certain circles as once
Achilles among Trojans was referred to as
      The Heel.
      Note cards, three by five, made
a private hoard, modesty a triumph over
      flagrant calls for print or lecturing.
Each month he found it harder to believe
      in general application. The arm was now
          unique.
He left in his will, provision for a minor
      edifice, an unassuming mausoleum,
          the arm as Monument,
to be entirely sealed, to stand without a sign.
      From the earth it would rise as if it were,
          had always been
            a part.

the Women

        stand around,
their hands out
        for something
to drain out of
Marilyn Monroe's hair,
        so they can eat it,
keep it somewhere

But Marilyn went away,
        her hair went with her.
All she left was mist
        or a wind.

In a while that goes
        too

She

Cleopatra's face has been uncovered,
            unearthed upon
a coin. Plain.

The light of an aura,
She appeared before Caesar
On a frame of carpeting.

She was simple as Aladdin's lamp.
In her eyes, Antony
Slowly drowned.

By the ancients vaunted,
Her dusky voice calls through haunted caves,
Blown along the ambience of tongues.

Her day put her plain face to bronze,
Beer coins for grubby thumbs to rub.
            For love,
Homely men, plain women.
They lose themselves.

On Kurasawa's movie of *The Idiot*

Also in Hokkaido your eyes
          lived in your skull,
luminous, behind bars, as in a jail,
          each stone known.
You were presentiment of many things,
          you were hovering
much as wings do, or palms, over
          a bowl of light.
          Maybe your thin body
made a dim cape shutting out
          perpetual snow
as does paper. Goodness in you
          was live, though
          crippled, inarticulate.
You were felt as a winter warmth
          that itself is taken
at last into the gray, your
          eyes in their prison house
          closing down,
          a weariness

When

       the world
did not stick to me
like a fungus,
I could peel it off,
drop it at my feet,
lingering as a strip-teaser
or quick as a baseball hit
and put the door to,
close it like night,
an eyelid down the signboard.

      Go where

Our love lay
secluded as a bird's egg
in an empty church
before dawn
before the sun crept up
with his searchlight
to surprise us with nothing
but breath.
The bed and the room
kept mute
as the other world.
We believed, then,
returned there,
Simple as nightfall

Attrition in six episodes — multa media

Sue Bridehead tried, yearning to be
Forever the Companion, burning pure
Platonic for her keep

Modest compared to Jackie K.
Who contracted (they say)
Handsomely for same, plus name

Well, men are creatures.
They have their seasons
Which some reason will have their due,
Whatever the decor

Glowing with a pure white jet
Will move angels or Tinker Bell
Who touch no earth nor meat

The nitty gritty will pop up
Like a pink worm after a rain
In soil walked by English masons

As well as seafaring Greeks who
Try to fly but
Sink down to terra firma

Icarus found his marvelled wings
Gave way to the sun. The best wax
Runs

New foreign student

He makes up for his garble
        of English
with an armful of smile,
shows me his big fist of languages,
all of them exotic.
His Assyrian tome of dictionary
        is pure embroidery.
Semiramis visits his mind,
stray perfume from redolent Bagdad.

Still he is modern,
        an exile, wandering,
Picking the crumbs off our shoes.
He's escaped, oddly, a land
where Edward's the name of misfortune.
Sin hides in Christians, strung up,
a few, in the square, along
        with more numerous Jews;
            by Moslem edict.
Restricted these days,
    the Mohammedan heaven,
        the houris lumpish, ill-tempered,
            good up-to-date shrews

Crevice

It's not comfy riding
    the generation gap,
Being an Aunty looking in.
Nephew's with I Ching,
Digging organic yuck,
Along with buddies
    Building their own,
An oversized garage around
    a real fireplace which
They hope won't smoke
When they cook.
Already I get wind
    of the outhouse,
Fan the flies of regret
    from a compost pile
Also containing hunks I've long left.
Their lean youth, their hope, their
    ignorance will feed it.
For me it grows a squeamishness.
My girdle will not conceal my fat
Or my awkwardness straddling
    cynically, with sympathy
My half-assed liberalism

Short Rest

My daughter is asleep
    on the couch
Arm flung above her mahogany hair
Her nose, pure line,
    her face in shaded sleep
A long nobility.
After all these years I do not know
    how I could have shaped her.

She will soon go to a man.
    The date is marked.
Though I shall smile and make
    myself busy with festivities,
I shall swell with hollows,
    the unfairness of arrangements.
Let the indifferent suck philosophy.
I shall digest letters

Drowning

My life is pouring through
    a hole in my head
So fast
     I shall drown
       in its waters.
         Remembering's a broken dike
        When the Angelus sounds
          over the wastes
I rise
Stretch out,
    a field
fallow

Where am I

What am I doing here
in this place of ratatat
like a troubadour in a Ford plant?
    There's danger
I shall slip toward the conveyer,
    be swept on,
Inexorably, a spoke to a wheel,
        or
under a hood, never
    to be seen again.
Come, Rosinante, bend low.
On with my armor
    Together we shall amble through
        the open window,
and ride on pleasantries
    to disappear into
the green above Toledo

Reeds

My daughter is disappearing into marriage
         slowly
     like a girl pulled back
   by a Japanese movie camera
       receding
     into her long hair,
      her garment,
    walking into reeds,
      evanescence,
     in fog, clouds . . .
        mist

With us

World too much,
wordy willie boy?
    What you know about it
out there, then messing around
      with all them lakes?
      Today, it's bottoms on her Paul Revere,
      tomorrow, measure stairs for carpeting,
      day after, fixing all those there appliances
        so they apply.
Gimme, somebody, a plucked goose
    so I can see what goes free naked.
    What grows without work except hair.
Punching in each twenty-four.
    Not Willie.
    He dead.
Hippies got a great thing,
    dream,
        till squares got hold of it
        sat it in the barber chair
        for sideburns
        and trimming

Mature, mature

She's growing up,
　　　already the unpardonable things
are rushing at her as if they were dogs
　　　she'd whistled to.
Love thinned out lean as a telephone wire
　　　between poles of marriage and divorce,
　　leaving a long hum, a busy signal,
　　　repeating no dice, none, none.
Back she went to school to Master.
　　　　Out with one foot firm at the chalk line,
　　　　　crouching in the line-up at the tape,
　　　　　　pant under the smile,
　　　　　signal flapping,
　　　　　Vita, please.
The shot doesn't go off.
　　　　Vita's not enough.
They want your blood,
　　　this is the season for vampires.
Her skin's taut and sleek;
　　　not quite as soft.
　　　　Maturation—spine at the rope,
　　　between rounds, disappointments,
Waiting for the gong,
　　　lemon between teeth,
　　　　eluding the brute
　　　shooting from his corner.

the long runners

and we who struggled,
dragging our youth behind us,
arriving at the garden
to see the fruit enter
out of the tree, shining,
saw it shrivel then,
turn into rind,
our teeth falling on it,
wolfish from hunger,
the nourishment acid.
Our eyes burned betrayal,
dared not,
for mocking each other,
where could they look.
Our mouths parched our smiles.
Disappointment hurried its hidden
and dangerous vial through our veins.
Yet we danced, our marionette feet
burned to their points,
still at the lash of that tune.
We could not say loud
we were nubile on poison,
the purest visage now a starch of mask.
Remember this plainness of face,
But fast

Reprieve

The snow will come down late
    this year
Past Christmas now, the air's
    amber
Still with leaflessness
Stark trees flank the curb
    in stunned avenues
Boughs are spread into a dancer's arch,
    drop tears
 dense as ferns
Distance brings the gauntness out,
Leaving them the echoing appeal
    of aging actresses
Exhaling disappearance
Even the warmth seems to float past them
They wait, listening in the night
The wind hesitates,
               not long

door county

Here in this musty hick room
    out in the sticks
        the wind huffs and noses
    at the windows with its September rush of rain,
        dollops of water dropped out of a popped bag.
I'm alone in a twin bed sag,
    old vacations, mothballs moulding
        in distant heads.
Friends everywhere else signal once in a while
    with a far note from the seventh wonder
        of some world.
"Labor Day in Paris, I'll be there,
    and will you?"
I crumple the notes, bitter pill
    downed with hours we had last decade
        for a chaser.
With aftertaste. Swallow, and quick turn
    to the other bed draped in fog.
        "For God sake,
Please get out of that grandpa bed,
    come console me for what's frittered,
        what do I care
About the spheres in your book congruent
    at some point out where the stars meet?
Throw that cover, hold me near,
    your spheres are perfect enough,
        quivering for the here and now,
    Rarest bird."

To George

Even your name
            sounds strange,
                    disappearing
            round the gorge
Say it was an eon or yesterday
            when our bodies
Flashed
            in black waters of the lake
It must have been at least
            eleven at night,
That moon, round as a pizza,
            looking astonished at us,
All cheek
Certainly we were children,
            our love wide-eyed,
Agog with circus parades
            we made ourselves
    from skin and limb
The loveliest blare
            came sleek from our hides,
Calliope, inaudible
            except to us
That cop on the shore
            shook his fist
Till we giggled tremulos
            and swam out further.
Phosphorescence kept
            streaming away from us,
Fish magnified
And we laughed. Why didn't we
            swim on,
Meet the horizon,
            Shake hands with that moon
            I think
He would have taken us in

Processional

Four men come, top satin hats,
they walk through a dense garden.
From cypresses and hushes
floats a sapphire coffer.
It rests on a thin spire.
The men bow solemn, low,
and lift up the coffer.
The lid comes slowly open
to give a smoke wreathe spiral.
The fume curves in a woman,
clouds and a shimmer.
She hands the mirror high
to the clouds of the heaven.
They take up this child
of the woman called the night

Mr. Simpson

He had a gift, exquisitely trained
        for suffering.
I'll spare the beginning
    when mother snapped a rubber band
against his rompers and grinned
    around the braces on her teeth.

Leave it to say what he remembered
    from school was a whack on the knee.

Others tried, maintained he made
    his wounds himself.
They threw their scabs away,
    he preserved his by Egyptian embalming.

They buried carcasses of any kind
    below the ground
While his walked on with food and fife
    and amulets
To lead a brilliant after life.

He exercised his sorrows on parade
    until they showed
Quite a versatility for blowing up
    at any time,
Unannounced.

Too late he tried to pull the shade.
    The pressure blew.
Everything, but everything
    came through.

Vines

this man is wound
    around that woman,
who shows her glittering nails,
the children bask before the housemaid,
    she steals from the wife,
partners pry away a hand-raised building,
dish the father to an island, sere old age.
        Sacrifice is banished,
            wry for company.
        Each day is murdered honorably.
        Respect dies of scabs,
            Loneliness,
        a peaked fountain gurgling
            underneath
              traffic

Kin

Remember Orpheus
was of the same thin blood
as Lot's wife, both
from the flighty brood of laggards

She slipped into her backwardness at once
Frozen down to her original salt.
Sonambulary slow, he started, turned
And fumbled his dear vision
In the fraying dark.
Left with only his loneliness to pluck,
Harp-string nostalgia,
He felt in his wrist her throbbing heart,
The pulse between her breasts.

Lions he charmed in the forest
Gave cool admiration
Distant audience,

The remote sympathy of manes

Oh Noah lead me
Where can I find the Ark

That woman, that blousy prophetess,
    Jehovah's witness
        in the morning glory sun
        of the early Sixties
Warned
        there were twelve calendars
            till dust.
She was good-dowdy, glassy-eyed,
    ready, already to skip
        this mouldy pancake
        earth.
She rode the street
    delivering
        like a precinct banger
    flapping Armageddon
        on her lashes,
    pages of her truth Tower
        swirling oil-stained pigeons
    to the air.
        I heard her out,
            counted up.
The years, a dozen, have come,
        have gone.

These jackroller days we toe
    on holey sneakers
        switch on the neighs of Sheikhs.
From her crystal eye,
    Suleiman rides,
        the latest buckaroo
    in a somewhat altered sheet.
Occult rains in mummied lands
    green old mole defenders,
Bubbling harem eunuchs out
    of sudden pitch-black fountains.
New moon polishes the Star
    under Crescent glimmer.
Which slaves are more exalted
    as they fall,
        not upon a shield,
           hand-forged Damascus,
    but on mine and mortar.
        How swift the last eloping sand
into the gauze the houris hold
    in Paradise.

Question

I cannot think what holds me to you.
    If the earth could speak
        it might say that to the bind
          it spins on.
Something speechless, terrible,
    primitive is the cog
      that winds me.
If the far Aleut is tied to total white
    that might be passion
       if every other word were held under
        until drowned
  and its pummelled corpse floated out,
  only the pale print blabbing on the wet.
That might be something like.
Sometimes I see a pair,
    hand in hand through the wood,
    a clearing near,
      Beyond,
    a witch, her ginger house,
    her fires, and all that stepmother ice.
      I wish they told me only
        of a fairy tale.
And the path of crumbs, whatever
    happened to it, strewn
      among those gorging birds.
Hands were warm, groping their way
    in, out,
      without eyes,
  Moved only
    by the silent knitting of the stars

How Dare

you be the man you are
and not the one imagined?
What ho
you turned into a husband.
How speak of marriage
in the context
of contracts.
Lock me in a drawer
where I fight
for my life.
I was dreaming like Rousseau's tiger
in the tropic green,
you became the magic 1890 balloon
that would float me out.
That banging in the drawer
is my muffled roar.

on the Passing
of Daylight Saving

Night comes
Already winter with its barbed wire
    and witch weather
Stands in wait
Poised for our blindfold
    with gag and drop cloth.
The cars are threading home,
    sucking moans from the pavement.
Birds are still whooping it up
    on trees whose leaves whistle by,
silly as foolish grasshopper
    who fiddled his time like a cello—
as if tomorrow did not toss bread
    on the wave of departure.
The abyss of the gas oven poises
    like the ghost in armor
        returning at midnight
seeking revenge,
even justice.
At the word descending leaves
giggle their hysteric last
    down into the street.
Our hour is cut without notice
    by a frivolous tooth.

The world does not bend its bald head
        for a pat.
No insurance man pauses
        to scatter checks before the axe
                of the blind woodcutter.
Appalling winds will howl soon
        down the mouth of the beginner
                who grapples for the world's throat
        to hear it say Uncle.
Only the gangsters are good at this.
They used to carry their guns in cases
        shaped for violins.
No longer necessary.
The wolf is already here.
He owns the whole doorstep
        with a handsome number in brass
Soldered onto the long door-pull of his stay.
For him no changing neighborhood,
        his complexion is fixed.
This night will get only thicker,
        send poets to sprawl in their slobber,
The children keel over,
To the high titter of trees,
While shrill leaves are frisked
By the fist of the season

Nixon in Crisis

The headline sounds Greek
    His fate's determined
to linger like a dog-star,
    its clutch on the sky
cut deep enough so he could look
    a fixture of defiant nature,
blazon longer, defined from chance
    to send him out, hurtling
a great smoke toward infinitude,
    from comet of the year.

    Heaven's herald falls,
eclipsed by mystery or smog,
      Frog prince
back to original slime

Goodbye,
>> **on my birthday**

And when I go, this desk I leave you,
my navel, my grave,
>> my monument.
Let it stand in all of its
>> Silence,
Dishevelment rooted,
each of my likenesses,
Lips muted,
Papers turning their palms up,
lips pursed together,
not neatly, haphazard
as life, as if words by chance
fell over them, dust,
the dust of the bins on deposit,
kookiness, spread fins of my dance
clumsily shaking the air,
small hisses of various departures,
flips, leavings that never took off,
the advent that colored space neighbor,
some inadventure, as if a cloud
solidified slowly on wood,
busy-ness, all of the scratches,
gouges of pain into oak,
as if this head were delivered
one at a time of each separately,

miniscule, the groan of each fraction,
no more pompous than the slick
cast over the floor,
secrets of mounting euphorias,
dolls, multiple creatures,
gorgeous as gorgons grooming
their way up to be unicorns,
        shanks, horns, goggles, apparitions
pearly with sheen, and
langorous rubies cooling their rays
on quartz floors in a grotto through
green murmurs of waves,
all this out of the old maw
in the oaken fixture, this desk
reproaching never, quiet, waiting,
a guest assumed to be prudent

In the park

    a curious sympathy
    emanates
from statues.
there's the city founder
    here.
one time I could sit
    unaware at his feet.
I can't go close anymore.
    Once youth is gone
      there's a bond
    laid between these hulks
      of stone,
    their nameplates known
      or not.
They tell us they're waiting,
    we'll be in their shade
      with nothing to remind
        anyone.
No birthday card for me this year.
I said I didn't care—a lie.
    A yearn at last for ancestor
      observances ?
We are statues, premature
    our only sacredness,
      where
          ?

Travelogue

The man is perhaps a beanstalk
lurching against this film backdrop
and not particularly lucky
since it's not a story,
even though these craggy peaks
with their dusky velvet
caress the eyes almost shut.
The sun will disappear by
falling down behind quite
unobtrusively as a servant
masterminding everything into
a magical evening coming up . .
Everything for the man to delight in
if only, if he had the wherewithal,
if these mountains offered themselves
to him instead of standing off,
overwhelming colored rock he must conquer,
he must or die in some part.
Now he looks like a peapod, nudges
himself to pull together,
first he must square his shoulder,
since a hero stands without fear.
He is no wild flower in the cranny,
The chance was wrongly presented,
the time was time he had not,
he lifts his feet, they look like leaves.
Wait, just let him find a place
to sleep, my God if he got out of there . .
A sign hangs on the falling sun,
Time and rock wait for no one

cold autumn

the sea wails
and flails its dragon tail
into a froth
white fire on jaws
of sand

we were there
in each other's arms
our mouths, our ears
were drugged
the hours whisked their
lilting foam
we scarcely heard

years melted in water
magnetic roar inside
a shell held up
and listened to

your slender sand
spills out
through glass

Enlightenment

She starved two whole days
in the ashram after instruction,
her carrot curls disheveled,
her sari awkward from her hands
that were clever but American.
She waited, waited for her blue eyes
to shoot satori bolts of clear
illumination, till tears, whole
puddles spilled along her nose.
Complaints she whispered were wilting
offerings to her guru. He curtly
ordered, 'Go eat your supper.'
She took the next flight home
without hesitation, angry,
his holy phrase was no chute
to the ineffable.
  Buddha could suffer years
and shrug. American time was hard coin
  off in far Bombay.

Ash

The second wife
of my first husband
keeps turning up
unexpectedly,
odd decades,
worse than a
bad penny.
A little fake you can
palm off,
a ghost is indestructible,
does not require a mantel.
Even in hell
I shall confront her
rounding a turn,
rising inexplicably
from her own smoulder

Troy, about the fifth year

Before these nagging walls,
   everything drags on, on,
   this war which was supposed
   to be over, still limping.
   Bread, water every day.
   Home rings in my ear
   till I can hardly hear what's there.

My wife, will she want me?
   I won't look in clear water,
   I must look like the dog my father
   used to keep for the sheep.

Damn Helen, it was to skip over,
   skip right back. If I was young
   as Leander, I'd sneak off
   in the drink. Wonder if home
   won't turn out to be this
   blandly curling shore.

Kite Away

A piece of luck —
you got away
   completely
from the boy holding you down
  by your string.
Into the rushing air
  you took a free ride
on the side saddle of wind.
Your mane is exulting.
Even birds have to strive
  with their wings.
You flew clean,
  minus fare,
  minus pain.
No sweat, kite.
  Everything deserves
at least one free ride.
I see you still bobbing way up,
flinging your leash over wires,
  over trees
past all the windows, their caged-in
  faces tracking you,
waiting to see what you get by with.
  Ah, you snagged,
hardly visible, your long anchor lead
clamped on a tiny weather vane,
  on a top spire.

Well, that vane pays for its keep,
    going round and around,
    strictly aground of its tower.
Wouldn't you know he'd get you,
    whirl,
while you're going to crumble and tear.
Not many soar as far, even for kites,
    nor escape the obvious,
to be foiled at last by a small
    and metallic bird,
right on the job, as if by
        envy.

Falling,

almost asleep working
dull clauses for
dull tomorrow,
I saw the cut of a wing,
heard a mocking cry,
'What are you doing there
on the flatland, away from
the salt fling, fins of the waves.'
The sea gull veered, fading away.
Waking, looking out to night shadows
holding the foreheads of buildings
around their gaunt brows,
their yellowing speechless windows,
silences piling up like layers
of mattresses waiting for weariness
to bed itself,
there waits tiredness beyond sound.
It's a beggar before trees mute
with an inwardness beyond loan.
That gull is the life, one
with insatiable hours,
drifted into that land,
its locked murmuring sea
they belong to.
Outside of these walls
dense with fortresses,
I turn,
ask of these trees who only
stretch

Swallows

She scurries to keep the dark out,
   fencing chaos from her window box,
with a fabric tried with many colors.
   At fifty, her supple hands seek out
the light from lone peripheries.
   Solitary hands could always mould
a balm against strangelings
   in somber alleys of her years.
   Years lambent for her always
radiated from a man. With him
   the hands could lull a while, subdued,
then turn for their common enterprises.
   She could never comprehend
the flurried energies she burned
   as sacrifice to him, mulling love,
then chafing sodden embers.
   The same with every man. Loneliness,
again, hands like swallows in
   a prevailing wind, darting over
paints and dies, metal, wood and clay,
   relentless wings, swooping from a spell.
To praise of her work, she apologizes,
   it seeming a slender talent, taken in
as foundling. What she is or ever wanted
   flutters opaquely inside, beating back
      incessant on itself

ding

This poet I met told me
he's giving up the world,
going to dig in himself,
drilling for buried treasure.

Much later I saw him,
Inquired.
It seemed he'd come up
for air for good.

The drilling made him dizzy,
    and the sawdust
Wasn't anything negotiable.

Blackbirds

I tread a ragged line
to balance my eggshell head
between my careful shoulders
Of late my head's been wearing thin
from restless abrasives
Sometimes I feel under my scalp
four and twenty blackbirds
pecking their way out
My hair, it rises, begins to walk
Head, Emerging Blackbirds
What a dainty dish
to set before the king,
sending a flurry different
from pure John before Salome
Each bird will sail out
on the ample ozone,
floating an arc,
ballet swimmer in water,
each curving down on a circular veer,
falling, dipping, banking,
hovering in an undulant frieze
slower and slower
paling wholly away
till the air does not stir
The King on his throne
reels with looking
wall-eyed bronze
Only I, patting my hair down
know where they've gone

Snow Quiet

Snow
is falling
    quiet
    steady
as if the world
were a bird
whose tail
God is pouring
salt on
so that it will
come to him.

Even if it's doubtful
    the world
will come to him,
    he keeps
bending over
    salting

vellum Offset, basis 60. The book was composed, printed and bound by P.T. Printing Company, Chicago.

This book was set in souvenir light 11 point, with 3 point leading. Text stock is Scott Vellum Offset, basis 60. The book was composed, printed and bound by *P.T. Printing Company*, Chicago.